POPERY

AND THE

UNITED STATES,

EMBRACING AN ACCOUNT OF

PAPAL OPERATIONS IN OUR COUNTRY,

WITH A VIEW OF

THE DANGERS WHICH THREATEN OUR INSTITUTIONS.

By RUFUS W. CLARK, M.A.
PASTOR OF NORTH CHURCH, PORTSMOUTH, N. H.

BOSTON:
PUBLISHED BY J. V. BEAN & CO.
NO. 21 CORNHILL.
1847.

In the interest of creating a more extensive selection of rare historical book reprints, we have chosen to reproduce this title even though it may possibly have occasional imperfections such as missing and blurred pages, missing text, poor pictures, markings, dark backgrounds and other reproduction issues beyond our control. Because this work is culturally important, we have made it available as a part of our commitment to protecting, preserving and promoting the world's literature. Thank you for your understanding.

POPERY AND THE UNITED STATES.

WHILE we do not belong to that class in the community which foresees in every hostile movement or popular outbreak, the certain downfall of our institutions; neither are we disposed to regard the present strength of our government, and prosperity of our nation, as certain evidences of stability, and continued success. The same care which was exercised in laying the foundations of the republic, and the same vigilance which was manifested by our ancestors in guarding the virtues and promoting the intelligence of the people, must not only continue to be employed, but must be increased in proportion to the magnitude of the dangers that surround us.

That vigorous, extensive and skilful efforts are made by the friends of popery to establish among us the supremacy of their system, and thus arrest the progress of free principles and the Protestant faith, no one can doubt; but in regard to the result, there is, even among the best friends of our institutions, a diversity of opinion. Some, who have examined the subject, and travelled over the land, and observed the actual progress and workings of popery, assure us that we are in imminent danger of coming under its sway. Others, whose opinions are entitled to respect, declare that we have no occasion for alarm; and even where popery is advancing, it assumes so mild and modified a form, that we have nothing to apprehend from its prevalence. If, however, we will look at the facts in the case, and understand definitely the nature of the system, the actual advancement which it has already made among us, and the character and extent of the exertions which are put forth in this country and in Europe for its promotion, we can form our own opinion of the question of danger, and of the importance of this subject in its bearings upon the welfare and destiny of the most interesting nation upon the globe.

We would not indulge in the spirit of boasting, nor overrate the importance of our national career; but the conviction grows upon us every day that, in the providence of God, this rapidly advancing republic is destined to perform no inferior part among the nations of the earth.

Mighty elements are at work among us. Among them, are our prodigious growth within so short a period, the spirit of far reaching enterprise and indomitable energy which pervades the mass of the people, the fact that the most civilized nations of Europe are pouring their population upon us, and the anomaly of so young a people sending out their Christian influences to the most benighted regions of the earth, and undertaking the stupendous work of elevating, intellectually and morally, the whole human family. All these, together with the inevitable extension of our national territory and power to a degree perhaps unparalleled in the history of the world, give to our country an interest and importance which cannot fail to impress every enlightened and philanthropic mind. The bearing, therefore, of so formidable an evil as popery, cannot, and ought not to, be overlooked. In the present-discussion it will be our aim to present as impartial and correct a view as our sources of information and the nature of the case will allow.

We propose to measure the strength of the evil as it has developed itself upon our soil; to compare the elements of Romanism with those that enter into our political, social and religious institutions; and to suggest the method in which the foe should be met and vanquished.

After the discovery of this continent, the various nations of Europe had the opportunity, by establishing colonies here, of testing the power of their different institutions to originate new nations, and secure their success. While the states of our Union, with the exception of Maryland, Louisiana and Florida, were settled by Protestants, or those professing no peculiar religious tenets, the whole of South America, Mexico, and a portion of the Canadas, were settled by Roman Catholics. The latter, besides having obtained a vastly greater extent of territory than the Protestants, had decidedly the advantage of them in the richness of their soil, salubrity of the climate, mineral resources, and all the physical elements which contribute to the growth and prosperity of a people.

Spain, at the time of the conquests achieved by Cortez, Pizarro and other distinguished generals, was at the height of her power; and was capable of rendering the most important aid to her colonies. But it was not long before the powers of Europe began to perceive, that the experiments of Protestantism and popery, as elements of civilization, were fast developing the strength of the former and the weakness of the latter. The nations founded by the Romanists seemed destitute of enterprise; and not only a spiritual, but a political, deadness pervaded them. In the arts and sciences, in commerce, manufactures and internal improvements, they made little or no progress. They have had their revolutions as well as we; but their changes of government have been little better than throwing off one yoke, to receive another equally galling and oppressive. Even at the present time, their republics are rocked by internal convulsions, and the mass of the people is degraded by ignorance and vice.

The progress of our own nation in wealth, power and intelligence, not only excited the jealousy of the adherents of popery, but presented inducements to emigration, even to Catholics, greater than those of any other nation upon this continent. The papal powers, therefore, instead of confining their attention to their own territories, have directed their eyes and their efforts towards us. The movement, which at the outset was feeble, has become a mighty struggle on their part to overthrow our institutions, and thus bring the whole continent under their sway. And they have attacked us at a vulnerable point, one where our armies and navy can be of no avail, and one which it is not in accordance with the genius of our institutions to protect by intolerant laws. They are aware, as well as we, that it is our religion which has made us to differ from the other American republics,— that it is our Protestant faith which has given us strength to cope with the mightiest nations of the earth, which has developed with such unexampled rapidity the resources of the land, which has to such an extent promoted education and general intelligence, which has sent our commerce to every sea and unfurled our flag in every port, which has made our influence felt in every court in Europe, and which has enabled us while conquering one nation to feed the starving thousands of another. Hence they feel confident if they can succeed in overthrowing Protestantism, that our political and social institutions must also fall, and the days of our prosperity and glory be numbered.

As the result of their efforts, they now have in our land a population of at least two millions. Some put the number as high as three millions; but as we have no official reports upon which perfect reliance can be placed, and as their numbers are so rapidly increased by immigration, it is impossible to state with precision their numerical strength.

From the Catholic Almanac for 1847, published in Baltimore, we learn that there are in the United States two archbishops, twenty-three bishops, one vicar apostolic, eight hundred and thirty-four priests, and eight hundred and twelve churches. Since these statistics were compiled the number of priests has greatly increased. It is but a short time since there arrived at New York, in the packet ship Havre, one bishop, twenty-eight priests, and six nuns; and it was stated that twenty-nine other priests were on their way in the packet ship Splendid. The steamer Portland recently landed in Boston nine papal priests in a single day; and within the last six weeks forty-nine have reached the same port. From the twenty-first of April to the twenty-seventh of June, inclusive, seventy-four thousand one hundred and eighty-four immigrants arrived at New York, the great majority of them being Roman Catholics. Thousands, too, are pouring into Philadelphia, Baltimore, and all the other principal ports on the Atlantic. By comparing the statistics made up last year with those of 1837, we find that, since that period, the number of dioceses and bishops has doubled, and the number of priests has more than doubled, while the number of churches has tripled.

In their schools and colleges they have nearly twenty thousand pupils, more than one half of whom are Protestants! A great proportion of the teachers in these institutions are Jesuits, the bitterest foes of civil and religious liberty who breathe the air of heaven. Their attention is chiefly bestowed upon their female seminaries, as they have sagacity to see, that, if they can get the control of the female mind of the nation, and through this operate upon the coming generation, they shall ultimately succeed in their designs.

In the diocese of Cincinnati, which embraces the state of Ohio, there are the ecclesiastical seminary of St. Francis Xavier, the St. Xavier College, three convents, four female seminaries of a high order, and eight or ten charitable institutions. Among the latter is St. Peter's Orphan Asylum and Free School, at Cincinnati, containing ninety-five female orphans, and from one hundred and fifty to two hundred other pupils under the care of six Sisters of Charity. There is also the St. Aloysius German Male Orphan Asylum, which contains forty orphans. The Aloysian Schools of the German Congregations, taught by four Catholic schoolmasters, at an annual expense of sixteen hundred dollars, contain five hundred children.

St. Joseph's Convent, in Perry Co., Ohio, is the *oldest Catholic institution* in the State, and has served as a nucleus around which the papists have gathered. We are told that " recently several talented and exemplary fathers, from the sunny climes of Italy and Spain, have come to aid their brethren this side the Atlantic: so that with renewed energy and promptitude, the fathers can now devote themselves to the cultivation of the extensive portion of the vineyard entrusted to their care."

In the single diocess of Louisville, comprising the State of Kentucky, there are forty-three churches, ten chapels, two ecclesiastical institutions, two colleges and *ten female* academies, besides four female religious institutions, and four charitable institutions. In the convent of the Sisters of Charity of Nazareth, there are eighty professed sisters in the community, most of whom are devoted to teaching. Sisters of Charity conduct the Female Academy of Nazareth, at Bardstown, which is a very flourishing institution, — St. Catherine's Female Academy, the Female School of St. Vincent of Paul, and the Female Academy of Louisville. In this day school the number of scholars is from seventy to one hundred. In the basement of St. Louis Cathedral, there is a free school for girls, under the charge of three Sisters of Charity, having one hundred and twenty pupils. Within this same State, there are but two Protestant female seminaries of a high order; and in the State of Indiana there is not one which will at all compare in importance and prosperity with the Catholic seminaries. Consequently the Protestants, in multitudes of instances send their daughters to the Catholic schools; and when remonstrated with, their excuse is, that there are no good Protestant seminaries for young ladies.

Nor is this the state of things simply in these dioceses to which we have referred; the same is true of nearly all the Western States, according to the testimony of intelligent and truthful witnesses. In the state of Missouri there are eight convents, seven academies for young ladies, and eleven schools. Now let it be remembered that these institutions are established and conducted by men who are the bitter and uncompromising foes of general education, and whose sole object in teaching in this land is to instil into the youthful and unsuspecting Protestant mind the errors of popery. If this is not their design, why do they take such unwearied pains to get the children of Protestant parents? Why do not the societies in Europe, the Leopold Foundation, and those at Lyons and Paris, send Jesuit teachers to South America and Mexico? Why do they not open schools in Italy, Austria, Spain, Portugal and Ireland, those strong holds of papacy where so deep an interest is felt for the youth of our land? In those countries they have no need of schools; for the mass of the people is already safely bound in the chains of spiritual despotism. The papal church has resorted to education only to advance its interests; and not to impart light and instruction to the mind. Of its success in the use of this instrument, we have a striking example in the manner in which the Lutheran reformation was arrested, when in the full tide of success. Scarcely had forty years passed away, before this reformation had sent its purifying and life-giving streams over every part of Europe; so that even in Austria almost the entire mass of the people, embracing all classes, were claimed as Protestants. The ministers at the altar, the professors in colleges, the teachers of academies and schools, had nearly all abjured the Catholic faith.

The Emperor of Germany, being hostile to the reformation, formed the design of checking it by means of education; and calling to his aid Ignatius Loyola, the founder of the order of Jesuits, he assured him that "the only way to prop up the decaying cause of Catholicism was to give the rising generation pious Catholic teachers." This plan was entered upon and pursued, until the Jesuits obtained the control not only of all the higher seats of learning, but also of the common schools; and through these, they not only arrested the progress of free principles and vital religion, but rolled back the tide of the reformation almost as rapidly as it had advanced. Mr. Ranke, in his History of the Popes, speaking of the astonishing results of this measure, says: "This is a case without parallel in the history of the world! All other intellectual movements which have exercised an extensive influence among mankind, have been caused, either by great qualities in individuals, or by the irresistable force of new ideas. But in this case the effect was produced without any striking manifestation of genius or originality. The Jesuits might be learned, and in their way pious: but no one will affirm that their acquirements were the result of any free or vigorous efforts of mind. They were just learned enough to get a reputation, to secure confidence, to train and attach scholars; but they attempted nothing higher." Yet by strict method, untiring diligence, and union of effort, they succeeded in their designs; and much of the strength that the Romish church gained by that movement it retains to this day. In speaking of Ignatius Loyola, and his order, Mr. Macaulay, in his usual forcible and impressive style, remarks: "His activity and zeal bore down all opposition: and under his rule, the order of Jesuits began to exist, and grew rapidly to the full measure of its gigantic powers. With what vehemence, with what policy, with what exact discipline, with what dauntless courage, with what self-denial, with what forgetfulness of the dearest private ties, with what intense and stubborn devotion to a single end, with what unscrupulous laxity and versatility in the choice of means, the Jesuits fought the battles of their church, is written in every page of the annals of Europe during several generations. In the order of Jesus was concentrated the quintessence of the Catholic spirit; and the history of the order of Jesus is the history of the great Catholic reaction. That order possessed itself at once of all the strong holds which command the public mind,—of the pulpit, of the press, of the confessional, of the academies. Wherever the Jesuit preached, the church was too small for the audience. The name of Jesuit on a title page secured the circulation of a book. It was in the ears of the Jesuit that the powerful, the noble and the beautiful breathed the secret history of their lives. It was at the feet of the Jesuit that the youth of the higher and middle classes were brought up from the first rudiments to the courses of rhetoric and philosophy. Literature and science, lately associated with infidelity or with heresy, now became the allies of orthodoxy.

"Dominant in the south of Europe, the great order went forth conquering and to conquer. In spite of oceans and deserts, of hunger and pestilence, of spies and penal laws, of dungeons and racks, of gibbets and quartering blocks, Jesuits were to be found under every disguise and in every country,—scholars, physicians, merchants, serving-men, in the hostile court of Sweden, in the old manor-houses of Cheshire, among the hovels of Connaught; arguing, instructing, consoling, stealing away the hearts of the young, animating the courage of the timid, holding up the crucifix before the eyes of the dying."

Now it is this same order, under their present general, Father Rothaan, a man of great shrewdness, energy and resources, which is laboring with such zeal and success in our land. Their leader in the Western States is the President of St. Xavier's College at Cincinnati; and they are pursuing the same policy here, which was pursued with so much success under the reign of Ferdinand in Germany. Through their ecclesiastical seminaries, their colleges, their convents, their female academies, their asylums, their free schools and their manual labor institutions, they are seeking to infuse their opinions and doctrines into the minds of the rising generation. And who will say, that these institutions, at the West are exerting no influence, and that we at the East shall never feel their power! It is true, that we have our own colleges and schools at the West, and that Protestants are doing much to evangelize the whole nation; but it is also a melancholy truth, that, in many sections of the land, popery has of late years advanced more rapidly than Protestantism. Catholic churches have multiplied faster, their schools have been more prosperous; and although they have gained but few proselytes, yet, what is of more importance to them, they have been silently, yet steadily, obtaining a powerful influence over thousands of youth and children.

On the continent of Europe, there are four societies organized for the purpose of propagating the Catholic faith in the United States and in Canada. Of these societies, the Leopold Foundation in Austria, is one of the most prominent. This association has been in successful operation for about sixteen years; and has expended during that period two hundred and ninety thousand dollars. It is under the special patronage of the Emperor of Austria, and its business affairs are transacted in Vienna. The government which sustains it is the most perfect military despotism in the world; and is a prominent member of the so called Holy Alliance, which is leagued against the liberties and rights of the people of Europe. The subjects, from whom the funds sent to us are extorted, are the most abject slaves, physically and morally, upon the continent. And the only conceivable motive for the establishment of this, and similar societies, is to extinguish the light of freedom which has blazed up upon this continent, and whose beams threaten to dissipate the darkness of popery, and to enlighten the millions who have so long bowed to its sceptre. These societies not only aid the colleges and churches to which we have referred, but contribute liberally towards the erection of churches and cathedrals; and are ready to assist in any way towards the extension of the Catholic faith among us. And it is worthy of remark, that it is a principle with the priests in this country not to part with real estate which may come into their possession. The remark has been frequently made by them at the West: "We purchase land, but we never sell it."

So great has been the increase of Romanism in our land, and so sanguine are the friends of the system of the ultimate triumph of their principles here, that not long since twenty-six bishops met in Baltimore; and in their Convention had the presumption and impudence to pronounce these United States a province of the Pope at Rome! This land of civil and religious freedom, of revivals, of benevolent institutions, of Bibles, of Puritan principles and faith, proclaimed to be a portion of the dominions of the greatest political and ecclesiastical tyrant who lives upon the earth!

But let us compare the elements of Popery with the principles which lie at the foundation of our institutions.

In the first place, as a political system, popery is, and ever has been, the bitter foe of freedom. Despotism is a quality inherent in the very texture of the fabric. There is not, and never has been, upon the face of the earth, a papal community which has not been deprived of its rights, denied the full privilege of suffrage, and trodden in the dust, by the worst forms of tyranny. By the power of the confessional, that most formidable of all engines of oppression, the very thoughts, desires and emotions of the mind have been read by the ecclesiastical and civil authorities. By means of the knowledge thus obtained, and the mastery thus gained over the people, papal governments have been enabled to carry out their designs, and protect themselves against all opposition.

For proof of the correctness of these remarks look at the past and present condition of catholic countries, and more particularly at Italy. If the papal church is what it pretends to be, the only channel through which the favors of God are communicated to earth, and if the Pope is the viceroy of Heaven's King, then we should naturally look to the dominions immediately under his cognizance, and the objects of his special care, for the most striking exhibitions of the blessings of civil and religious liberty. But what is the actual state of Italy at the present time, after having enjoyed for twelve centuries all the advantages that popery could confer? Intelligent and truthful travellers assure us, that nothing that greets the eye, wears the mark of enterprise or happiness. On the other hand, decay, deterioration and wretchedness are stamped upon the face of the whole country. The government over which the so called vicar of Christ presides, is made up of injustice, extortion, intrigue, and the worst elements of despotism. Virtue in the subject is no protection, and innocence no safeguard. Trials for crimes committed against the state are conducted in secret; and not unfrequently, it is far preferable to suffer private injuries, rather than resort to the law for redress. Men of property or talents are the objects of constant jealousy and suspicion, and are liable at any moment to feel the grasping power of their priestly rulers. All stimulus to distinction out of the church is taken away, and even all the departments of enterprise and trade are monopolized by the priests. Then, as an additional burden to the people, they are obliged to support an immense army to keep them in subjection. If one breathes of discontent, or gives utterance to the faintest desire for freedom, he is liable to be arrested. If a community confer together with reference to improving their political or social condition, soon bayonets and swords are glistening among them; and the least movement towards rending asunder the chain by which they are bound, is at once suppressed. Through the corruptions of the confessional, domestic happiness is invaded; and the tenderest relations of life are made subservient to the base designs of a priestly despotism. Nor is the condition of the people any better in Austria, or Spain, or Portugal.

Now these Jesuits and their adherents, who are laboring in our country, would substitute this despotism for our liberty, this desolation and these blasted hopes for our prosperity, these obstacles to labor and industry for our spirit of enterprise. They would overthrow our government, to put in its place one which will rob the nation of its growing power, obstruct the channels of business, scatter the seeds of discontent, anarchy and wretchedness, and bring the nation down to a level with the papal countries of Europe. And this they are striving to accomplish, not by the power of argument from their pulpits, not by the splendor of their cathedrals, or the attractions of their worship, (although there is no lack of these means,) — but mainly by educating the rising generation, and by gradually obtaining the control of the ballot-box. The course pursued by Loyola and his followers, after they had gained sufficient influence, and prepared the way by education, was, to avail themselves of the aid of the civil government, and complete their work by forcing into submission all who would not yield to persuasion. And the same policy would the Jesuits pursue with us to-day, had they the power. They have repeatedly confessed as much; and although they are now silently and cautiously pursuing their work, yet they are full of sanguine expectations that the day is at hand, when they shall be strong enough to strike the decisive blow. And they are urged on by the principle of self-defence, as well as by the desire to extend their system. They feel that they have more to fear from this nation, than from any other upon the globe. They know that our free principles and Protestant faith will continue to work their way among the victims of superstition and oppression in Europe; and they are acting under the conviction that they must either conquer us, or be conquered. In this view they are correct; and would Christians in this land *do their duty*, not only would all danger from Popery be removed from our soil, but we might evangelize the entire continent of Europe, dissipating the deep darkness that enshrouds her deluded millions, and shattering into a thousand fragments those iron systems of despotism with which they are cursed. But we have too much evidence that Protestants are not doing their duty in this matter; and our solicitude is awakened as much by the apathy of the friends of freedom and of pure Christianity, as by the skill, industry and resources of our opponents.

Another point of contrast between this system and our own is, that while our religion makes its appeals to the intellect and heart, popery addresses the external senses, and acts upon the superstition of its followers. It seeks not to enlighten the understanding, and purify the heart, and elevate the affections, and desires and purposes of the soul; but keeps the mind in ignorance, and acts upon its love of show and vain ceremonies. Its priests, professing to be heralds of the truth, fear nothing so much as the truth; professing to lead souls to Christ, their instructions are the greatest obstacle to true conversion. Instead of promoting religion in the heart by the light of God's word, and the influence of sound argument, and the example of a holy life, they depend upon relics, and superstitious rites, and the decrees and dogmas of corrupt councils. At the exhibition of the holy coat at Treves, in 1844, said to be the veritable seamless garment which our Saviour wore, we have an illustration of the power of superstition over the minds of these deluded people in this nineteenth century. During the seven weeks that this garment was exhibited, it is estimated that over twenty thousand persons daily visited it, and the ceremony was continued amid the ringing of bells, the roar of cannon, and every manifestation of public rejoicing. As the pilgrims approached the garment, some would devoutly prostrate themselves before it; others would pray to it for the pardon of their sins; and all would cast their offerings into the treasury. The sick were brought to be healed through its efficacy; for they believed that it had imbibed the bloody sweat of Christ's agony in the garden, and had been refulgent with celestial glory on the mount of transfiguration.

Besides the coat, the cross on which our Saviour expired, the spear with which he was pierced, and the table at which the Supper was instituted, are preserved and exhibited. There is a church where the very foot-prints are shown, which St. Peter left impressed upon a marble pavement, when on his way to Rome. In another, is said to be the altar at which he said mass; and in another, the chains which he wore when in prison. A fourth, contains the cradle in which the infant Jesus was rocked; and in a fifth, may be seen the stairs of Pontius Pilate, which Christ ascended. There are thousands of bones, defaced pictures, and other trifles, which are regarded as sacred relics, and viewed with more reverence than the atonement itself. On certain days, too, the solemn farce is enacted of bestowing the priestly blessing upon horses and cattle, and upon the fields and crops.

Missionaries and money are pouring in upon us, to establish here these same mummeries and superstitions. For our pure gospel, the Romanists would give us their baptized Paganism. For our revivals, they would substitute pilgrimages to Baltimore or Cincinnati, to witness and worship a piece of some old garment. For our liberty of conscience, they would give us the iron laws of ecclesiastical despotism. For our charitable societies, they would substitute monasteries and nunneries. Indeed, the wrath of the Pope has already been poured out against our benevolent societies, and particularly against our associations for distributing the Bible; and it is our firm belief that any form of vice, or any calamity, would be endured in Italy with more patience than a Bible society. The appearance of a wasting famine, such as is raging in Ireland, or of the Asiatic cholera, or an outbreak of profligacy that would make virtue a hissing and a by-word, would not cause greater dismay and pious horror among the ecclesiastics at Rome, than the organization of a Bible society in the imperial city. Let a committee wait upon Pope Pius IX, who now occupies the chair of Peter, and solicit his acceptance of the Presidency of a Bible society, and let the six cardinal bishops be elected vice-presidents, and one of the cardinal deacons be made secretary, and the fifty cardinal priests, who constitute a part of the council of the Pope, be made life-directors by contributions from the Leopold Foundation; and let there be erected under the shadow of the dome of St. Peter's, a Bible house, with its steam-power presses, and its fonts of type, to print the sacred scriptures in Italian, Spanish, French, and Portuguese; and let the use of the church of St. Peter be requested for the purpose of holding the first anniversary of the society, and Pius the Ninth would, in our opinion, be more pious than any of his predecessors, if he did not open fresh vials of his wrath, and issue his bulls, and rain down his curses more copiously than they ever fell upon the head of the monk of Erfurth, Martin Luther, or any of his followers. The Bible and Popery! They can no more be assimilated than can light and darkness, or truth and error. As well might we think of establishing prayer-meetings in the halls of an Inquisition, and associating converting grace with the tortures of the rack.

We have abundant evidence of the hostility of papists to the Bible, in the efforts already made to exclude it from our common schools, and in their care to keep it out of the hands of their people: and the Jesuits, no doubt, design to give us, in time to come, still farther and more emphatic proof of the same feeling.

We might, did our limits allow, institute a comparison between the Catholic clergy and those of the Protestant faith, and point out the notorious infidelity and profligacy of many of the former, and particularly of the ecclesiastics at Rome; we might refer to the zealous efforts that are made to destroy the liberty of the press in papal countries,—to the suppression of the liberty of speech, to the spirit of bitter persecution that popery has, in all ages, manifested, to its union with the state, to the corruption of its nunneries, and the sad revelations of the confessional; but we cannot tax the patience of our readers by a full discussion of these points.

We have seen enough, however, to convince us that a deep, systematic, and extensive plan has been adopted, and is now in progress, to overthrow our institutions, and bring this nation under the blasting and withering influence of Romanism. Nor has the world ever witnessed a more gigantic undertaking for the production of evil, and the destruction of good, than is presented by this conspiracy against the liberties and religion of these United States. When we consider what this republic has done, and is now doing, for the extension of freedom, for the spread of the gospel, for the promotion of general education, and for the removal of the various forms of human wretchedness, we want language to express our indignation at that base and fiendish undertaking which is aimed against our government, and contemplates the establishment of the curse of popery upon this Protestant soil. Nor was there ever a more strange spectacle presented to the world than that, — while thousands and tens of thousands of the inhabitants of papal countries are flocking to our shores, to enjoy the benefits of our institutions, — the emissaries of the Pope should be laboring to extend here that pernicious system which, in proportion to its prevalence, will make this land so much less an asylum for the oppressed. The simple reason why Catholics are crowding to this Protestant land, is because they cannot live under their own system; and every one can see that, if that system prevails here, their condition among us will be as intolerable as it was at home. Could they leave behind them their bishops, priests, and Jesuit teachers, they might come here with the anticipation of permanently enjoying the blessings of our free government and Protestant faith; but by bringing these enemies of liberty and pure religion with them, they are like persons who, in escaping from an infected district to a healthy region, carry the disease with them, and thus pollute the pure atmosphere, which might have insured their health.

It is, indeed, wonderful, in our apprehension, that the question should not suggest itself to the intelligent Catholic, as he steps upon our shores: "Why have I come to this Protestant land? Why have I left the home of my fathers, the scenes of my childhood, the church in which I was educated, and come to spend the remnant of my days with heretics, — with those whom I have been taught from my infancy to believe were my bitterest enemies, and the vilest of the human race? Have I been banished to this infidel and anathematized land for my crimes? Am I unworthy to enjoy the blessings which Popery confers in those regions, where for ages it has held undisputed sway?" But so blinded are even the most intelligent, that such reflections scarcely ever occur to them;

and while cherishing their prejudices, and laboring to extend Popery here, they do not seem to be aware that they are doing all in their power to destroy the blessings they have come to enjoy.

But we hasten to speak briefly of the manner in which this evil is to be met.

It would be contrary to the spirit of our government and religion to pass laws excluding the Papist from the privileges of our institutions, or to resort to any form of coercive measures to arrest the progress of Romanism. Liberty of conscience and liberty of opinion are principles which lie at the foundation of our republic. The only instrumentality, therefore, which we would employ, is *the power of truth*. Let the Scriptures be circulated; let religious tracts and books be greatly multiplied, and placed in every family in the land; let intelligent and pious teachers be sent forth to counteract the influence of the Jesuits at the West, and let the gospel be preached in its purity and power, and the expectations of the Romanist here, in regard to his supremacy, will never be realized. We have read with what eagerness Luther seized the Bible which he found in the library at Erfurth, how strongly he was excited by the consciousness that he held in his hand the Word of God, and with what indescribable feelings he turned over the leaves of the sacred book, and drank in the rich truths there revealed! We have read how the light from that single volume gradually spread, and grew brighter and brighter, until it extended over Germany, Sweden, Denmark, Scotland and England; and we can trace the fruits of that excellent translation of the Scriptures which Luther made into German, and which for three centuries has supplied that people with the bread of life.

Now our dependance for the protection of our civil institutions and puritan faith is upon the same precious volume, and especially upon having its principles instilled into the minds of the rising generation. And if this work is ever thoroughly done in our land, it must be done speedily. Romanists are crowding upon us faster than they can, with our present means, be instructed and supplied with the bread of life. They are inundating many portions of the land, where the field is clear before them for establishing their own institutions and systems of education. Nor does it need a prophetic eye to discern that, in the future, emigration from Europe will be greatly increased. Our ship-loads of gratuitous supplies of food which have gone forth, are cards of invitation to the destitute and oppressed, which will be accepted by thousands and tens of thousands. They will reason that if there is such abundance here, and such benevolence as to prompt our citizens to send hundreds of tons of food the distance of three thousand miles to strangers and foreigners, how much more would they find relief in the country itself;* and being disgusted with their own governments, and discouraged by the injustice and oppression to which they have been subjected, they will naturally spend their last farthing to reach our shores. Instead, therefore, of the one hundred thousand which has been about the average for the last ten years, we may expect this year, judging from the number that has already arrived, near half a million; and it should not be forgotten, that there is at this moment surplus population enough in Catholic Europe to come here and out-vote the Protestants at the ballot-box.

The evil, therefore, which we have been considering, if it has not already assumed a formidable aspect, is one which is destined, in a very few years, to make its power sensibly felt in our land. Of this no intelligent observer can for a moment doubt; and the longer we slumber over this subject, the greater will be the probability that we shall awake to a sense of our danger when it will be too late to save the nation.

In comparing the relative strength of Popery and Protestantism in our land, it is important to remember that, while the Papists are united, and all bent upon the extension of their religion, those whom we denominate Protestants are divided; many of them being infidels, and a still larger number being indifferent to all religion; and from the disposition which some political parties have manifested to avail themselves, by compromise, of Catholic votes, to secure their ends, we cannot have that confidence in our numerical Protestant strength which our present majority would seem, at first view, to warrant. The true friends, therefore, of vital religion and civil liberty have duties to perform of a most weighty and pressing character. Let them be faithful, and our institutions, our freedom, and our Protestant faith are safe. But let them neglect their duty, and be recreant to the high trusts committed to them, and our worst fears with reference to the triumph of Popery will be realized.

* The ship-of-war Jamestown took out eight hundred tons.

Printed by Libri Plureos GmbH in Hamburg, Germany